The Magic of Sri Lanka

CONTENTS

Sri Lanka – A Mosaic of Culture and Nature   2

The Capital, Colombo   14

The Wildlife   16

The Cultural Sites of the North Central Plains   28

  Sigiriya, Rock Fortress Palace   36

  Polonnaruwa and Anuradhapura, Ancient Capitals   42

Kandy, the Hill Capital   54

  Temple of the Tooth Relic   62

The Highlands   68

  Nuwara Eliya   72

Bibliography   79

Acknowledgements   80

Sri Lanka – A Mosaic of Culture and Nature

Over the centuries, Sri Lanka has been described as a tropical paradise. This is hardly surprising, as it has everything – sun, sea, sandy beaches, cool mountains, ancient lakes, forests teeming with wildlife, precious stones, magnificent archaeological sites and, above all, friendly, well-educated people. Combine this with a good tourist infrastructure and it is not hard to see why it is such a popular tropical island destination.

Physically, Sri Lanka is a teardrop-shaped island in the Indian Ocean, separated from the Indian peninsula by the Gulf of Mannar and the Palk Strait. It measures 432km from north to south, and 224km from east to west. Fine sandy beaches can be found around almost the

entire coast, although it is the strip from the west coast to the south, with its sandy bays and delightful coves, that is the most heavily developed for tourism. The resorts at Negombo to the north of Colombo and those to the south at Bentota and Beruwela are magnets for beach lovers and watersports enthusiasts. Further south are Unawatuna and Hikkaduwa beaches, which are ideal for snorkelling and diving, where swimmers can share the ocean with turtles.

Around the southern coast are the Dutch fortress towns of Galle and Matara, and beyond these lie the sanctuaries of Kalametiya and the national parks of Bundala and Ruhuna (Yala). Here, the jungle belongs to elephants, leopards and dozens of other large animals. Tissamaharama, once the centre of an ancient kingdom, is now a thriving safari destination.

Sri Lanka's exciting mix of wildlife and culture is nowhere more evident than in the ancient capitals of the north central plains. Culturally, the ancient kingdoms of Anuradhapura and Polonnaruwa rival those of the Egyptians, Mayans and Incas, whose ancient religions have been lost. In contrast, many of Sri Lanka's ancient temples pre-date Christianity, and its Buddhist and Hindu culture is still very much alive.

Opposite Top: The area around Kandy is dotted with ancient temples, each decorated with stylized wall paintings.

Opposite Bottom: An ornate stone staircase is a reminder of the short-lived glory of Yapahuwa, the capital of King Buvanekabahu I, in the 13th century.

Above: Sri Lanka still holds many surprises, such as the Serendib Scops Owl (*Otus thilohoffmanni*), which was discovered by Deepal Warakagoda in 2001.

An early appreciation of aesthetics has given the island a wonderful legacy of beautiful sites, from the sublime rock-cut sculptures at the Gal Vihara in Polonnaruwa to the palace and gardens at Sigiriya. These are an early example of an organic movement within architecture, which was sympathetic to the surrounding landscape. Today, very little survives intact, but fortunately the remains include Sigiriya's famous frescoes of beautiful maidens that have provoked much debate.

Anuradhapura and Polonnaruwa form two points of a cultural triangle. The third, to the south, is the hill capital of Kandy. This became the seat of the Sinhalese kings when successive invasions and internal dissent led them to abandon the magnificent capitals in the north central plains. The route south to Kandy from the north central plains runs past the cave temple complex of Dambulla, and the Aluvihara in Matale. Unlike the kings, the monks never deserted their monasteries and continued to uphold the monastic traditions over an unbroken stretch of several centuries.

The ascent to Kandy takes you into a cooler climate, which can nevertheless seem sweltering in the hot season. Kandy is at the centre of the nation's Buddhist soul and has one of the holiest shrines in the Buddhist world. The Dalada Maligawa, or Temple of the Tooth Relic, houses a tooth of the Buddha, retrieved from his funeral pyre. Every year, the Esala Perahera, one of the most spectacular pageants in the world, is celebrated with over 100 costumed elephants and thousands of drummers and dancers taking to the streets.

The British, who finally subdued the Kandyan kingdom, set their sights higher and established the hill station of Nuwara Eliya up in the highlands. The journey up here takes you through mile after mile of tea plantations, which form green carpets that cover the mountainsides.

Opposite: A view of Yoda Wewa looking towards the ancient and sacred hills of Vedihitikanda. Yoda Wewa, meaning 'Giant Lake', is one of the many ancient man-made reservoirs that date from the southern Ruhuna kingdom. It is believed to be the Dura Wewa referred to in ancient inscriptions, which was built in the 1ˢᵗ century AD by King Ilanaga.

Above: A view of the enigmatic mountain of Ritigala. Legend has it that the Monkey God Hanuman brought a section of a Himalayan Mountain to Sri Lanka that was covered with a number of medicinal plants, in an attempt to treat Lakshmana, the wounded brother of Rama. The mountain section slipped from his grasp and landed at Ritigala and Unawatuna, creating two hills that are rich in health-giving herbs and plants, several of which are endemic species. Ritigala also has the remains of a forest hermitage, with a stone avenue leading up to it. There are several explanations for the name Ritigala. One is that it means 'rock as steep as a long pole,' another that it is named after the Riti trees in the nearby jungle. On the other hand, the island's ancient record, the *Mahavamsa*, calls the mountain Arittha-gala, which translates as 'dreaded rock,' perhaps because it was home to the fearsome Yakkas, the aboriginal inhabitants of Lanka. It is possible that over time, Arittha-gala became Ritigala.

Tea came at a price. Much of the island's biodiversity was lost; what little is left clings to the harsh mountaintops and ridges and a few protected areas like the Horton Plains National Park. Although much diminished in size, the highland plateaux and forests continue to be a refuge for many plants and animals found nowhere else in the world.

Above: Leopard Rock in Yala National Park is at the junction of several leopard territories. JRMC1 (pictured) was a sub-adult who briefly held sway, before he was displaced by one of the mature males.

Below: The Mirror Wall at Sigiriya (5th century AD) had an architectural function and also served as a tablet for travellers to inscribe poetic verse.

Opposite: There is a wide network of trails around the island, traversing forests, tea estates and ancient villages, which has established Sri Lanka as a destination for mountain bikers.

Left: Around Ratnapura, gem-mining pits can be seen by the main roads. The Sri Lankan Government retains all mineral rights and prospectors have to pay a licence fee to mine for them (even on their own property).

Below: Dehideniya is a traditional village in the Hunnasgiriya area, near Kandy, where people turn brass sheets into intricate, exquisitely beautiful items, using special hand tools.

An ancient network of footpaths criss-crosses the island, making it ideal for trekkers and cyclists who wish to explore off the beaten track. The best-known trails lead to the sacred peak of Sri Pada, or Adam's Peak. For centuries, pilgrims of all religious denominations have made their way through dense rainforests (and now tea estates) and the cloud forest on the upper reaches of the Peak Wilderness Sanctuary to pay homage at the shrine on the peak.

One trail begins at Ratnapura, the city of gems. The gravel beds around Ratnapura are rich in precious minerals, making Sri Lanka one of the world's top five producers of gemstones.

Above: At Pelmadulla, the scrub forests that once harboured elephants have given way to large sugar cane plantations. It has been argued that it would have been cheaper for Sri Lanka to import the sugar and preserve the land for wildlife.

Below: Keselwatte is a self-sufficient hamlet in Hapuwida village – a place almost exclusively devoted to making lacquer-painted wooden artefacts.

Left: Devil Dancing masks have their origins in occult exorcism ceremonies. They have been adapted over the years for folk dramas, and more recently, souvenirs.

Above Top: With over 1,000km of coastline, the marine fisheries industry provides a source of employment for tens of thousands of coastal dwellers and a source of food.

Above: Friendly children are ever eager to pose and smile for photographers.

Overleaf: Morning at Cloud Forest, Horton Plains National Park.

The Capital, Colombo

The country's business capital, Colombo, has a mix often found in developing countries of five-star hotels and luxury apartments competing for land with slums. The city, like much of the country, once derived its wealth from trade winds that brought merchants and adventurers to its shores in search of spices and wealth. Today, its urban sprawl continues to spread ever outwards, smothering the countryside in a pall of pollution and traffic.

Above: Colombo's skyline keeps changing as the city becomes a busy metropolis. An unlikely gateway to rainforests, its location on the west of the island is strategic in providing access to the island's unique bio-diversity. A mere 100km away, in the lowland rainforests, is the Serendib Scops Owl (*Otus thilohoffmanni*). It was discovered only as recently as 2001 by Deepal Warakagoda, one of the country's top wildlife and birding tour leaders.

Aside from the name, there are no remains of the old Portuguese fortification built in Colombo. In the area there are well preserved examples of facades from the English colonial period (**Opposite Top**). These are in stark contrast with modern facades (**Opposite Bottom**), some of which use their frontage for advertising, at times creating the appearance of a huge, outdoor, pop art gallery. Security restrictions in Fort resulted in the Navam Mawatha area around the Beira Lake (**Left**), blossoming into the new hub of the city.

We
stand
strong
you
stand
out

We
strive
you
thriv

The Wildlife

Sri Lanka's wide range of climatic zones has resulted in distinct endemic sub-species, and the whole island is a complex and fascinating laboratory for studying the processes of evolution and speciation. The key to this diversity is its topography, which comprises a mountainous core in the southern half, fringed with scrub jungle in the lowlands, which in turn is edged with sandy beaches, lagoons and estuaries.

Above: The Sri Lankan Leopard (*Panthera pardus kotiya*) is a sub-species found only in Sri Lanka. The island is your best chance in Asia of seeing this beautiful and elusive hunter.

Left: Glad-eye Bushbrowns (*Nissanga patnia*) are common butterflies in home gardens that are heavily shaded by trees and undergrowth and forested areas of the wet zone.

Opposite: The Little Green Bee-eater (*Merops orientalis*) is one of four species recorded in Sri Lanka from the colourful family of Bee-eaters.

With Galle becoming a gateway to the rainforests, they are increasingly easy to access. Traditionally, visitors had to make the difficult journey to Sinharaja, where both the roads and accommodation facilities are poor. It was nevertheless a trip well worth making, for Sinharaja's local Forest Department guides are well equipped for guiding eco-tourists and are good at showing birds, butterflies and mammals. Many visitors come away from rainforests disappointed that they have seen nothing but trees, which is why it is essential to take one of the local guides

or a competent naturalist guide arranged by a Sri Lankan tour operator.

For example, you might wish to spot Red-faced Malkohas (*Phaenicophaeus pyrrhocephalus*), which are discreet and unlikely to betray their presence easily. But a skilled guide knows to listen out for Orange-billed Babblers (*Turdoides rufescens*), with whom the Malkohas form a mixed feeding flock. Ignoring the distraction of the more vocal babblers, the guide will peer up to spot the furtive Malkohas clambering around the shaded mid- and upper canopy.

Walking in the rainforest at night, you are taken to another world – an aural realm in which every tree, liana and epiphyte seems to be filled with the calls of amphibians. They squeak, grunt, bellow and bark in their quest to find territories and mates. Evolution has served Sri Lanka with a wonderful range of amphibians, so much so that it may have a higher number of frogs than Costa Rica.

So much for frogs, but what of larger animals? According to the laws of classical bio-geography, small islands don't have large animals. But thanks to its geological history with the mainland, Sri Lanka is in fact the best place in Asia to see both leopards and elephants. The only surprise is that, so far, the Sri Lankan tourism industry has failed to fulfill the island's potential as one of Asia's top big game safari destinations. But with the launch of leopard safaris and elephant migration tours, that is beginning to change.

To the south-east of the island is Yala National Park, one of Sri Lanka's finest National Parks. Its range of habitats is such that 100 species of bird can be seen in a single day during the migrant season. In Block 1 of the park, research by Ravi

Opposite: The rainforests of Sri Lanka are amongst the richest in South Asia. Each tree is a community in itself, supporting climbers, lianas, mosses and algae, which, in turn, provide habitats for small animals.

Above: Mangroves are extremely important to support the oceanic food chain, which extends out to the deep ocean. Many marine species spend their early stages in and around mangroves. The destruction of these valuable wetlands causes long-term impacts on the health of marine fisheries.

Right: The success of rainforests lies in their efficient recyling of biological matter. Hundreds of fungi species can be found in the tropical forests, which gain their nutrients from dead trees and branches, helping to speed up the process of decomposition.

Above: The Ceylon Frogmouth (*Batrachostomus moniliger*) is a strange, charming, nocturnal bird confined to the forests of the lowlands and mid-hills.

Opposite: Family units in elephant society are dominated by females and often comprise a mother, daughters and perhaps a grandmother as well, which coalesce into larger family groups and clans. At times, these may number 100 elephants or more.

Samarasinha suggests that it may have one of the highest densities of leopards anywhere in the world. Given the open terrain of the park and the leopard's status as the top predator, the chances of seeing this normally elusive cat are high.

Leopards are found throughout the island and have been recorded in Wasgamuwa, Uda Walawe, Minneriya, and Maduru Oya National Parks, although they remain very elusive there. They also hunt on the roof of Sri Lanka, in the Horton Plains National Park, which is popular with day visitors: sightings are becoming more and more regular. The park has rolling grassy plains, perhaps from an ancient history of cultivation, interspersed with precious cloud forests.

In September and October, one of the great events in the international wildlife calendar occurs in the lowlands – an annual migration of elephants to the receding shores of the gigantic Minneriya Lake within Minneriya National Park. Food, water and shelter are available, and elephants gravitate towards them from the surrounding scrub jungles.

Although Minneriya is seasonal, elephants are virtually guaranteed year round in Uda Walawe National Park. It is safe to say that of the thirteen countries in which the Asian Elephant (*Elephas maximus*) is found, Sri Lanka offers the best chance of viewing them.

Opposite Top: The Palm Squirrel (*Funambulus palmarum*) is a widespread and common mammal, at home both in forest and in gardens. A pair of these animals is often found in the company of Yellow-billed Babblers (*Turdoides affinis*).

Opposite Bottom: Recent research has shown that Sri Lanka may have over 200 species of amphibians, yet to be described by science. If this turns out to be true, Sri Lanka could actually have the highest number of amphibians in the world. A remarkable diversity of rainforest species has taken place, in what biologists term an 'evolutionary radiation'. One reason for this is that these species of frogs develop into adults while still in the egg. This means they do not need the tadpole stage, common to other frogs, reducing their vulnerability to external conditions.

Right: Rhino-horned Lizard (*Ceratophora stoddartii*) is an endemic lizard found in the highlands of Sri Lanka. It can even be seen in well-wooded gardens in the Nuwara Eliya area. The horn is probably a way for males to establish their mating credentials, but its exact function remains a mystery.

Above: Giant Wood Spiders (*Nephila maculata*) are common in lowland rainforests. The small spider sometimes seen with a female is not a baby, but a male. This is an extreme example of sexual dimorphism – where there are distinct differences between the sexes.

Below Left: 177 species of dragonfly and damselfly have been recorded in Sri Lanka, almost half of which are endemic. The Dawn Dropwing (*Trithemis aurora*) is one of the commoner species, found in wetlands in the lowlands and mid-hills.

Opposite: The Green Garden Lizard (*Calotes calotes*) is found in the lowlands and mid-hills. Occasionally it may even be seen in gardens in Colombo, although lizards seen in cities are more likely to be the Common Garden Lizard (*Calotes versicolor*). Males turn their heads into a bright crimson when they are wooing females and warding off rival males.

Above: Polonnaruwa is one of the best places to observe primates. Here, the lowland races of the Purple-faced Leaf Monkey (*Presbytis senex*) and the Toque Macaque (*Macaca sinica*) can be seen with the Hanuman Langur (*Semnopithecus entellus*). They are relaxed in the presence of humans and their intricate social behaviour, especially social grooming, can be observed with ease. Many female Toques in Polonnaruwa have red faces.

Below: From August to September the 'Gathering', the world's single largest concentration of wild Asian Elephants, takes place at Minneriya National Park. As the lake there dries out, a lush grassland sprouts on the exposed lake bed, and elephants from scrub jungle around Trincomalee and Wasgomuwa National Park converge for the food and water.

Above: The Sloth Bear (*Melursus ursinus*) is found throughout the dry lowlands in Sri Lanka where significant areas of forest cover remain. Although it will eat almost anything, it is partial to termites. The absence of its two front teeth allow it to purse its lips and vacuum them in.

The Cultural Sites of the North Central Plains

Very few countries can boast of an ancient culture that has continued to flourish to the present day, as Sri Lanka can. The country's landscape, its monuments, its people and their customs are strongly interwoven with Buddhism, along with Hinduism, which arrived later.

Above: A number of stone inscriptions survive from the medieval kingdom of Polonnaruwa.

Left: A Naga Raja stone, at the Jetavanarama Stupa in Anuradhapura. The seven-hooded cobra is a common decorative motif and symbolizes the 'pot of plenty'.

Opposite Top: The annual Kandy Perahera continues a tradition which has its roots in ceremonies held in Anuradhapura to venerate the sacred tooth relic.

Opposite Bottom: Rajangana is believed to be the Hattikutchi Vihara, referred to in ancient chronicles, where King Sri Sangabo offered his head under self immolation. One of the buildings excavated at Rajangana, is an outstanding example of a Vatadage (Circular Relic House).

Sri Lanka boasts one of the earliest recorded histories in the ancient chronicle of *Mahavamsa*. The historical accuracy of this chronicle has been borne out time and time again by historians and archaeologists. In fact, it has provided a useful chronology for events throughout South Asia, and India in particular. It records history from 543 BC, the year the Buddha attained Nirvana, to the year 310 AD, although it was written down later (between 459 and 477 AD) by Mahanama. Various scribes continued Mahanama's work in what is collectively known as the *Chulavamsa*.

The ancient chronicles provide an honest account of the history of Buddhism, making no secret of the fact that it has not exactly followed the Buddha's teachings of peace and compassion. On the contrary, it is an intriguing story of subterfuge, ambition and war.

The original and most orthodox monastery was the Maha Vihara (the Great Monastery). Over time a schism grew and a more liberal sect founded the Abayagiri, following the Mahayana form of Buddhism. Royal patronage was for some time conferred equally to both; then, over the centuries, the fortunes of the rival schools waxed and waned, until the reign of Mahasena.

Mahasena favoured the Abayagiri to the serious detriment of the Maha Vihara. Via the Abayagiri leader, Sangamitta, the Maha Vihara was persecuted, its buildings destroyed and its valuables taken. Its monks fled to the province of Ruhuna for nine long years in exile. The king's close friends and ministers were shocked; one minister rebelled, and rallied an army to fight the king. The two parties were camped on the battlefield when the minister decided to take lunch with the king. Over a good meal the old spirit of friendship was rekindled and the two decided to cease hostilities. In a dramatic about-turn, Mahasena decided to support the Maha Vihara, and the monks were called back. The ambitious Sangamitta was left vulnerable, and was assassinated by a nun.

During the reign of Srimegavarama, in the year 310 AD, a princess brought the sacred tooth relic of the Buddha from Dantapura in India to Sri Lanka, smuggling it in her hair. It was kept in the temple of Dhammachakka and became an object of veneration.

During his two years in the country in the 5th century AD, Fa-Hien records that an annual procession was held to exhibit the relic to the public. Heralds announced the event across the country several days beforehand. This tradition continues today at the Esala Perahera, held in July and August in Kandy.

Perhaps the most conspicuous feature of the dry plains are the numerous man-made reservoirs, or wewas. The ancient Sinhalese were great hydraulic engineers, and the result is over 1,000 wewas, mainly concentrated in the north-central province. Famous amongst the wewa builders was King Parakramabahu, who decreed that not a single drop of water should flow to the ocean without serving mankind.

Left: The Lankatilaka (The Ornament of Lanka), a colossal brick structure, was built with a large standing Buddha, which reached 18m in height. Today the walls stand 17m tall, but the roof has fallen down.

The tanks, as they are known, allowed the dry plains to become the rice bowl of the country. A well-fed army constructed vast metropolises at Anuradhapura and Polonnaruwa.

Today, a visitor admiring the serene beauty of the Gal Vihara Buddhas might find it difficult to imagine the turmoil undergone by the ancient kingdoms as they finally succumbed to repeated Tamil invasions. For centuries, they lay swallowed beneath the advancing jungle tide. Now, a new generation of archeologists is busy carefully unearthing the past.

Opposite: An intricately carved guardstone at the entrance to the Vatadage (Circular Relic House) at the Quadrangle in Polonnaruwa. The arts reached a zenith in ancient Polonnaruwa.

Above: Kaludiya Pokuna has the ruins of an ancient forest monastery, located near Mihintale, where Buddhism was first introduced to Sri Lanka. The caves in the forest are still used by monks.

Following Pages: The Lankatilaka has bas-reliefs on its walls, lending the appearance of extra storeys, which may depict the vimanas (houses of the gods). The ancient chronicle, *Mahavamsa*, described Lankatilaka as 'A charming image house... adorned with ornaments of flowers and creepers and with figures of Gods and Brahmas and embellished with buildings, with turrets, grottoes, apartments and halls'.

SIGIRIYA, ROCK FORTRESS PALACE

If there is one place that leaves a deep impression on visitors, it is Sigiriya. Its dramatic story centres around Prince Kasyappa, the son of King Dhatusena (459–477 AD). Being the King's son by a non-royal consort, Kasyappa executed his own father to gain the throne. The Crown Prince, Mogallana, fled to India in fear of his life. In order to protect himself from future attacks from the rightful king, Kasyappa made Sigiriya his capital and built a palace on the summit of the rock. He then proceeded to use his artistic genius to create a vision of heaven on earth, making landscaped gardens with water pools, fountains and terraces.

Below: On the summit of Sigiriya is a rock-cut pool. This was the centrepiece of the palace gardens that some archaeologists think were once here.

Opposite Top: An aerial view taken from the rock shows the extensively landscaped water gardens around its base. Sixteen centuries on, the plumbing of the water gardens still works. Sigiriya typified a form of 'organic architecture', where man-made structures are adapted around natural topography.

Opposite Bottom: In the 5th century AD, King Kasyappa moved his palace to Sigiriya, concerned that his half-brother Mogallana would avenge Kasyappa's killing of their father. The resulting complex was designed as both a refuge and a pleasure garden city; today it is one of the most astounding archaeological sites in Sri Lanka.

Above: The Sigiriya Frescoes depict what are believed to be Apasaras or celestial maidens – a common feature in religious and royal art in Asia. What survives today is a small fragment of what was once a vast art gallery.

Opposite Top: Natural caves on the rock were utilized as dwellings or as meditation cells by monks. A 'drip ledge' was often carved on the edge to prevent rainwater from flowing inside the cave along the roof.

Opposite Bottom: The mirror wall at Sigiriya is famous for the poetic verses left by ancient travellers – tourists, who visited Sigiriya after it was abandoned, mainly between the 6th and the 10th century AD.

Following Pages: Mid-way up the rock is a small plateau, which holds the Lion's Staircase. This is considered a masterwork of the bricklayers' and plasterers' art. All that remains today are the paws of a giant lion, which was a gatehouse to the summit. The steps ran inside the lion's body, which was made of brick and sculpted plaster.

POLONNARUWA AND ANURADHAPURA, ANCIENT CAPITALS

In the 10th century AD, the capital of the most powerful kingdom in the island shifted from Anuradhapura to Polonnaruwa, because the latter was in a better strategic position; it remained the capital from around 993–1250 AD. The Cholas from India were the first rulers here, followed by the Sinhalese King Vijayabahu I. The greatest king of Polonnaruwa was Parakramabahu I (1153–1186 AD). In his reign, the whole area flourished. Agriculture reached its highest peak and Sri Lanka became the 'Granary of the East'.

King Parakramabahu I (12ᵗʰ century) founded the Utararama, or Northern Monastery. He is remembered as one of the greatest kings of Sri Lanka. The Galvihara (literally 'Stone Temple') found here, contains some of the finest works of medieval rock sculpture.

There are three figures of the Buddha in this group: the Standing Buddha (**Opposite Top & Right**) show the Buddha in a posture known as animisalochana – giving thanks by standing in front of the Bo Tree, which sheltered him, whilst he meditated under it, to attain enlightenment. The reclining Buddha (**Opposite Bottom**) is almost 15m in length.

Below: Intricately carved stone columns supported the roof of King Parakramabahu's Council Chamber, while the walls are decorated with stone carvings of elephants and other animals.

Above: The Council Chamber of King Nissankamalla, the last king of Polonnaruwa to have ruled the whole of Sri Lanka. The columns along the inner nave record the name and title of the minister who should sit alongside it.

Opposite Top: A moonstone at the base of the entrance to the council chamber. The moonstone is believed to symbolize samsara – the endless cycle of re-birth and the path leading to Nirvana.

Opposite Bottom: At one end of the council chamber is a lion throne. Governor Gregory, a British Governor, had it brought down to the National Museum in Colombo. It has since been returned to its original location.

Following Pages: The Buddhist monument (stupa), Rankot Vehera, was built by King Nissankamalla in the 12th century. It is the island's fourth largest stupa.

Above: Sri Lanka is the best place in the world to see the Asian Elephant (*Elephas maximus*) in the wild. Not surprisingly, there is a long historical association with the animal: it has been integrated into the arts, cultural pageants and, in ancient times, even into warfare. The Council Chamber of King Parakramabahu I, is one of many examples featuring bas reliefs of elephants.

Left: A Guardstone at Vijayabahu's Palace depicts two common decorative motifs at entrances to royal council chambers and religious buildings.

Opposite: Anuradhapura is spread out over tens of square kilometres. The brick foundations and stone columns are all that remain of many religious and secular buildings. Their size and spacing give an insight into the former grandeur of the ancient capital.

Above & Opposite Top: Over 1,000 ancient man-made lakes dot the countryside in Sri Lanka's dry lowlands. They may seem randomly located but, in fact, are sited carefully along a hydraulic gradient, forming a series of water catchments. The water is transported between lakes through a sophisticated system of canals and sluices, and taken downstream to irrigate paddyfields.

Opposite Bottom: The Ruwanveliseya or Maha Stupa is one of the most important stupas in Anuradhapura. It was begun by Dutugemunu, the legendary warrior king in the 2nd Century BC. It stands 90m tall and is the third of the three largest ancient brick structures of the world.

Left: A monk leads the chanting of Buddhist verses in Aukana. The 12m-high standing Buddha here is in the abhayamudra (assurance) posture.

Below: A Buddhist nun offers her prayers at the Sri Maha Bodhi or the Sacred Bo Tree Shrine. This is the oldest historically documented tree.

Opposite Top: Medirigiriya is a monastery that is known for the outstanding Vatadage (Circular Relic House), which is perhaps the best preserved rotunda of this nature found in Sri Lanka. It is attributed to the 8th century AD, based on ancient chronicles.

Opposite Bottom: The Abayagiri Stupa and Monastery were built during the reign of King Vattagamini Abhaya (Valagamba) in 89–77 BC. By the 1st century AD, the Abayagiri monastery had become famous, attracting scholars from all over the world. Abayagiri enjoyed a golden age in the 3rd century AD under King Mahasena. At the site are the Twin Ponds, or Kuttam Pokuna, which are two unusual baths beautifully constructed in polished stone. The entrance steps to the baths have two stone punkalas (pots of abundance).

Kandy, the Hill Capital

Kandy is Sri Lanka's second largest city but quite different from Colombo, thanks to its hilly location and cooler climate. What we know as Kandy today was the ancient capital of Senkadagala. The name Kande, the root of the modern name, was derived from the Kanda Uda Pasrata, from the Sinhalese for the five counties of the hills. The city's four centuries of history have been a saga of courage, cultural renaissance, debauchery and treachery.

By 1505, the Portuguese had arrived on the Sri Lankan coast, and struggles for succession between kings now had the added factor of a European presence. During the reign of King Senarat, the Portuguese entered the city and destroyed much of it. The next to ascend the throne was Rajasingha II, a skilled warrior who engaged the Portuguese in two decisive battles – the first in 1630, when he routed them at Randeniwela. Peace was short-lived, and in 1638 the Portuguese destroyed the capital, but this was closely followed by a battle at Danture, where Rajasingha enjoyed his second victory and the invaders were defeated.

To strengthen his defence, Rajasingha II formed an alliance with the Dutch. But given their common interests in the cinnamon trade, it was only a matter of time before the Dutch themselves invaded. This began in 1659. In three years, the king lost what he had recouped from the Portuguese in twenty years, and Dutch troops burnt the palace to ashes. However, Rajasingha fought two important battles in 1665 and 1675, defeating the Dutch and winning back his territories.

Between 1760 and 1766, the Dutch battled with King Kirti Sri Rajasingha, who refused to sign a peace treaty and withdrew from the city, taking the tooth relic with him. The Dutch entered the city and plundered it, leading the Sri Lankan king to seek help from the British, who showed little interest in the matter at the time.

On the death of his brother in 1781, Rajadhi Rajasingha ascended to the throne. He was wary of the British and kept his distance, although he agreed with Governor North that the Dutch were a common enemy. He died in 1798. In the same year, the British gained control of the maritime provinces from the Dutch and were in a strong position to take over the entire island.

But the seeds of destruction were ultimately sown not by the British but by the Kandyans themselves with their petty disputes, jealousies and personal ambitions. Rajadhi Rajasingha died without children, leaving a succession struggle behind him. The crafty prime minister Pilimatalawa, who aspired to the throne, appointed Kannasami, an 18-year-old distant relative of the king, as Sri Vikrama Rajasingha. But the king was suspicious of Pilimatalawa and they both sought relations with the British.

Sri Vikrama Rajasingha sought to hold power by creating enmity amongst his own chiefs so that they would not unite against him. On one hand, he punished chiefs who had been unjust, and won popularity with the masses; on the other hand, he moved the sacred shrines of Natha, Vishnu, Kataragama and Pattini to Peradeniya from Kandy, which angered the Buddhist public.

Opposite Top: The lotus flower is a favourite decorative motif in temple art.

Opposite Bottom: Gallengolla Pothgul Raja Maha Viharaya is one of many ancient temples dotted around the Kandy area. The temple, like many others, is adorned with wall paintings.

Above: Columns in temples in Kandy are often decorated with carvings; the most celebrated carvings are located at Embekke.

Meanwhile, the British governor, Sir Robert Brownrigg, was biding his time. When several British merchants were taken as spies and mutilated, and a village under the British control was torched, he took the opportunity to declare war. Sri Vikrama Rajasingha was captured and sent to Vellore in India.

Opposite: Elephant sculptures decorate the walls of the Lankathilake Temple. The temple was built by King Buvanekabahu IV in the 14th century.

Below: The most celebrated wood carvings in Sri Lanka are on the wooden columns at Embekke. The temple is believed to have been constructed in the 14th or 15th century and to have been the audience halls of the Gampola kings. It was later converted as a temple of the Sinhalese war god Kartikeya.

The Sinhalese chieftains who co-operated with the British hoped that once the tyrant was deposed, one of them would be appointed king. But the British had other ideas. On March 2nd 1815, representatives of the two sides had a momentous meeting at the council chamber in Kandy, where they signed a convention. Under its terms, Sri Lanka became a British territory and the King of Great Britain became its sovereign. After four centuries of war with European powers, the island was handed on a plate by its own chiefs to the patient and tactical British.

Opposite Top: The oldest building in Kandy, the Natha Devale complex, dates from the 14ᵗʰ century, when it was built by Vikramabahu III. It is dedicated to the god Natha who is also identified with the Bodhisattva Avalokiteshvara. The Natha Devale is an Indian style gedige, and the Dravidian architectural style shows the influence of India's Vijayanagar Kingdom.

Opposite Bottom Left: The Temple of the Tooth (Dalada Maligawa) is one of the most famous Buddhist shrines in the world. The original temple was built by King Vimala Dharma Suriya I in the 16ᵗʰ century to house the Tooth Relic when it first came to Kandy.

Opposite Bottom Right: Solicitors advertise their services in a Kandyan street near the courts of law.

Above: Situated on the periphery of the Knuckles Range, Hunas Falls Hotel is a convenient base for submontane forests. It epitomizes many hotels in Sri Lanka, offering a luxurious and convenient base for discerning wildlife tourists.

Following Pages: Terraced paddy fields on the road through the sanctuary that has been declared around the Victoria, Randenigala and Rantambe dams. The drive is one of the most beautiful in Sri Lanka and conspicuous for the lack of roadside settlements along much of the way.

TEMPLE OF THE TOOTH RELIC

The Sacred Tooth Relic, housed in the Temple of the Tooth in Kandy, is an object of veneration to Buddhists and the most important object of worship in the country. From ancient times, kings have kept the relic in their kingdoms as a symbol of power. History records that it was first brought to the island by Prince Dhantha and Princess Hemamali during the reign of King Kirti Sri Meghavanna (301–328 AD). It is a traditional belief that whoever takes possession of the Tooth Relic, ruler or invader, has the power to govern the people.

Above: A royal attendant carrying a fan is set out in relief inside a wall of the former palace of the last King of Kandy, which is presently used as the Archaeological Museum.

Opposite: The first temple built to house the Tooth Relic was erected in the 16ᵗʰ century under the orders of King Vimala Dharma Suriya. The temple as it stands today, owes much to the renovations carried out under the reign of King Narendra Singha, several decades on. The moat, gateway, drawbridge and Octagonal Room were added by the last king of Kandy, Sri Vikrama Rajasingha. The Octagon Room or Pattirippuwa was built as a resting place, and is believed to be the work of Devendra Mulachari, a famous craftsman. At present, the Octagon Room houses an Oriental Library, which contains a valuable collection of Ola leaf manuscripts.

Above: The spectacular, and world-famous, Esala Perahera is held in Kandy for ten days every July and/or August (depending on the lunar calendar). A procession of magnificently-dressed elephants and dancers, the pageant is depicted in a contemporary painting on the walls of the Temple of the Tooth.

Opposite: Intricately painted and carved doors are found inside the Temple of the Tooth.

Following Pages: A head-on view of the Temple of the Tooth, or Dalada Maligawa.

The Highlands

The conquest of the highlands happened relatively recently, in the 19th century. Although scattered settlements existed, it was the British who pushed their way in with roads and railroads. This was not done in the spirit of exploration, but for money. The colonizers tried to turn the forest-clad mountains into coffee plantations; when coffee was wiped out by blight, they switched to tea. Ceylon Tea remains one of the most sought-after teas.

Opposite Top: A few species of tree ferns are found in Sri Lanka, some of which are unique to the country.

Opposite Bottom: A view of Adam's Peak (Sri Pada) from Horton Plains National Park, the roof of Sri Lanka.

Above: The famous 'Ceylon Tea' is harvested by hand. Almost all the tea pluckers are women of Indian origin.

Right: The 98m-high Devon Waterfalls and the 80m-high St Clare waterfalls are in close proximity to each other. Sri Lanka has many waterfalls because the island is formed of three steps or peneplains, which means that rivers often have to plunge down vertical drops as they make their way to the sea.

Following Pages: The Peak Wilderness Range rises from the lowlands near Ratnapura to a plateau averaging 600m. Within it are some high peaks including Adam's Peak (2,224m) the most famous peak in Sri Lanka on account of its religious significance. The footprint at the top is venerated by all. Buddhists believe it is of the Gauthama Buddha, Hindus believe it belongs to Shiva, the Christians and Muslims believe it is that of Adam.

NUWARA ELIYA

Nuwara Eliya is a bio-diversity city that is a good base for a number of cloud forest sites including Bomuralla, Horton Plains National Park, Hakgala, Sitha Eliya and Nanu Oya. The town centre lies at the foot of the Mount Pedro Forest Range, a cloud forest rich in endemic species: less than a few hundred metres away, for example, the island's top predator, the leopard, can be found.

In complete contrast are the gardens in Nuwara Eliya, replete with introduced horticultural varieties (**Opposite**). Many private home owners and the Municipal Authorities tend their gardens with a lot of love and care, maintaining a horticultural tradition acquired from the British from the 19th century onwards.

Naturalist Lal de Silva, takes children on botanical walks in the ground of St Andrews Hotel (**Below**). Some plants found in formal gardens, such as the *Lobellia nicotanifolia* (**Right**) are native species, found only in India and Sri Lanka.

Above: The Hakgala Botanical Gardens, a few kilometres from Nuwara Eliya, is popular with visitors. It is also one of the best places to see the highland race of the Purple-faced Leaf Monkey (*Presbytis senex*) and the Toque Macaque (*Macaca sinica*). The Toques brim with self-confidence: here a male approaches a human visitor to engage in a little inter-species dialogue. Visitors should take care, though, as the Toques are temperamental and aggressive. An attempt initiated by a human to get this close could lead to an attack.

Opposite Top: St. Andrews Hotel in Nuwara Eliya is a Tudor style, colonial property that is over 115 years old. It maintains the British horticultural tradition and continues to win many awards at garden shows. Recently, it has created a very small wetland reserve at the back of the hotel to provide a sanctuary for native species of plants and animals.

Opposite Bottom: The road from Hatton to Nuwara Eliya passes through some of the most famous tea estates on the island. Tea was introduced to Sri Lanka in 1849 after the coffee plantations were damaged by blight, and is now the island's second largest export.

Above: About 7km from Nuwara Eliya, near Hakgala, is the Sita Amman Temple. It is the only temple in Sri Lanka dedicated to the worship of Sita, famous from the Ramayana epic. The priest performs a daily pooja (prayer) and venerates statues of Rama, Sita and the Monkey God Hanuman.

Opposite: After the 99km post on the main Colombo to Kandy Road (A1) there is a hairpin bend at Kadugannawa. To the south-west of it, is a flat-topped rock known as Bible Rock, or Pathili Gala, an erosion remnant, which offers stupendous views across the countryside.

BIBLIOGRAPHY

Culture & History

Chandra Richard de Silva: *Sri Lanka A History*. Vikas Publishing, Delhi, India (1987).

Nimal de Silva: *Kandy A World Heritage*. City Deveco Designers & Publishers, Colombo (1994).

Anuradha Seneviratne: *Polonnaruwa Medieval Capital of Sri Lanka*. Archaeological Department of Sri Lanka (1998).

Anuradha Seneviratne: *Ancient Anuradhapura The Monastic City*. Archaeological Department of Sri Lanka (1994).

Wildlife

John & Judy Banks: *A Selection of the Butterflies of Sri Lanka*. Lake House Investments, Colombo (1985).

Matjaz Bedjanic, G. de Silva Wijeyeratne & K. Conniff: *Dragonflies of Sri Lanka*. Jetwing Eco Holidays, Colombo (2004).

Bernard d'Abrera: *The Butterflies of Ceylon*. Wildlife Heritage Trust, Colombo (1998).

T. de Fonseka: *The Dragonflies of Sri Lanka.* Wildlife Heritage Trust, Colombo (2000).

Gehan de Silva Wijeyeratne, D. Warakagoda & Dr T.S.U. de Zylva: *A Photographic Guide to the Birds of Sri Lanka*. New Holland (2000).

Gehan de Silva Wijeyeratne (Comp., Ed., Phot.): *Yala, Leopards & Other Wildlife*. A Jetwing Publication, Colombo (2004).

Gehan de Silva Wijeyeratne: *Butterflies of Sri Lanka*. Jetwing Eco Holidays, Colombo (2004).

Gehan de Silva Wijeyeratne & D. Warakagoda: *A Checklist of the Birds of Sri Lanka*. A Jetwing Publication, Colombo (2001).

Gehan de Silva Wijeyeratne & L. Perera: *Shorebirds, An Artist in the Field*. Jetwing Eco Holidays, Colombo (2004).

John Harrison (48 colour plates by Tim Worfolk): *A Field Guide to the Birds of Sri Lanka*. Oxford University Press (1999).

Sarath Kotagama & Prithiviraj Fernando: *A Field Guide to the Birds of Sri Lanka*. Wildlife Heritage Trust, Colombo (1994).

S. Miththapala: *Mammals of Sri Lanka* (for children). Colombo: March for Conservation (1998).

W.W.A. Phillips: *A Manual of the Mammals of Sri Lanka*. Wildlife & Nature Protection Society of Sri Lanka, Colombo (1952, 1980).

Photographic Essays

Nihal Fernando: *Sri Lanka A Personal Odyssey*. Studio Times, Colombo (1997).

Devika Gunasena (Text by Tissa Devendra): *Sri Lanka the Emerald Island*. Lustre Press Pvt Ltd., New Delhi, India (1996).

THE AUTHOR & PHOTOGRAPHER – GEHAN DE SILVA WIJEYERATNE

With weekly appearances in the media, Gehan is one of the best known corporate personalities in Sri Lanka, and is emerging as a celebrity in wildlife and tourism. Gehan has contributed a number of photographs, articles and reviews to newspapers, journals and magazines in Sri Lanka and overseas. He has a 'page' in the *Lanka Monthly Digest* (*LMD*) and *Serendipity*, two of the monthly business and travel magazines respectively in Sri Lanka. He has authored and photographed a number of publications, some of which are listed in the bibliography.

Gehan graduated in Civil Engineering from Imperial College, London and qualified as a Chartered Accountant with Deloittes Touche Tohmatsu in London. He worked for LIFFE, Abbey National and Sumitomo Finance. In 1999, after 11 years of experience in the British financial sector, he returned to Sri Lanka and joined the newly-formed senior management team at Nations Trust Bank. Since 2001, Gehan has been CEO of Jetwing Eco Holidays (www.jetwingeco.com, gehan@jetwing.lk), the specialist wildlife and luxury travel subsidiary of Jetwing. He is also a Director of Jetwing Hotels, responsible for developing nature-based tourism. He claims that the only record of significance he has achieved in his life is the highest rate of absenteeism, when he was the President of the St Joseph's College Natural History Society. This does not seem to have held him back from leading a multi-faceted life as a writer, photographer, sound recordist, natural history popularizer and high-profile corporate personality.

Opposite: Fruit and vegetable vendors ply their wares on the main Colombo to Kandy road (A1). Almost all of the fruits on display have been introduced to Sri Lanka, especially by the Dutch.

Above: With weekly appearances in the media, Gehan is one of the best known corporate personalities in Sri Lanka, and is emerging as a celebrity in wildlife and tourism. He wears many hats as a writer, photographer, wildlife populariser and corporate personality.

First published in 2005 by
New Holland Publishers (UK) Ltd
London • Cape Town • Sydney • Auckland
www.newhollandpublishers.com

2 4 6 8 10 9 7 5 3 1

Publishing Manager: Jo Hemmings
Project Editor: Gareth Jones
Copy Editor: Gill Harvey
Designer: Tyrone Taylor
Cartographer: Bill Smuts
Production: Joan Woodroffe

Reproduction by Pica Digital Pte Ltd, Singapore
Printed and bound in Singapore by Tien Wah Press (Pte) Ltd

ISBN 1 84537 110 0

ACKNOWLEDGEMENTS

Many people have assisted me over the years in my quest to discover my homeland, Sri Lanka. Most notably I must thank my wife Nirma de Silva Wijeyeratne and my friend Lester Perera, who have been such patient fellow-travellers while I insisted on taking a look at every ancient temple or forest patch. The introduction is drawn from an unpublished piece I had written earlier and extracts are used in this book and in another for Shoebill Publications. The essay on wildlife is heavily based on a piece for *Discover Sri Lanka*, a Sri Lanka Tourist Board publication, and is used with changes with their permission. It is thanks to the efficiency of my team at Jetwing Eco Holidays (www.jetwingeco.com), and my other colleagues in Jetwing, that I have time and space to describe and photograph the beauty of Sri Lanka.
My thanks also to Roland Silva, Vijita Silva and Tara Wikramanayake, who reviewed my manuscript, and last but not least, thanks to Hiran Cooray, friend, mentor and colleague – the only man in Sri Lanka who would have had the nerve to set me loose in tourism.